better together*

*This book is best read together, grownup and kid.

 akidsco.com

a kids
book
about

a kids book about

body image

by Rebecca Alexander

A Kids Co.
Editor and Designer Jelani Memory
Creative Director Rick DeLucco
Studio Manager Kenya Feldes
Sales Director Melanie Wilkins
Head of Books Jennifer Goldstein
CEO and Founder Jelani Memory

DK
Editor Emma Roberts
Senior Production Editor Jennifer Murray
Senior Production Controller Louise Minihane
Senior Acquisitions Editor Katy Flint
Managing Art Editor Vicky Short
Publishing Director Mark Searle
DK would like to thank Natasha Devon

This American Edition, 2023
Published in the United States by DK Publishing
1745 Broadway, 20th Floor, New York, NY 10019

DK, a Division of Penguin Random House LLC
Text and design copyright © 2019 by A Kids Book About, Inc.
A Kids Book About, Kids Are Ready, and the colophon 'a' are trademarks of A Kids Book About, Inc.
23 24 25 26 27 10 9 8 7 6 5 4 3 2
003-336889-Nov/2023

A catalog record for this book is available from the Library of Congress.
ISBN: 978-0-7440-8577-8

DK books are available at special discounts when purchased in bulk for
sales promotions, premiums, fund-raising, or educational use. For details, contact:
DK Publishing Special Markets, 1745 Broadway, 20th Floor, New York, NY 10019, or SpecialSales@dk.com

Printed and bound in China

For the curious
www.dk.com

akidsco.com

MIX
Paper | Supporting
responsible forestry
FSC™ C018179

This book was made with Forest
Stewardship Council™ certified
paper – one small step in DK's
commitment to a sustainable future.
**For more information go to
www.dk.com/our-green-pledge**

For Bella and Baby M.

Intro
for grownups

Not one single person is exempt from body image struggles. And yet, we rarely talk about these feelings with others. We feel alone in our insecurities. We feel like what's "wrong" with us is our fault.

We feel ashamed.

When we feel this way, very serious problems can arise. Eating disorders. Exercise disorders. Other forms of self-harm.

You were probably drawn to this book because you have a kid in your life, and because we all have bodies.

I hope this book will help you share the feelings you have about your body. I hope you'll talk about them with your kid. I hope you'll encourage your kid to do the same.

You might think you know
what this book is about,
but I think I'm going
to surprise you.

Yes, I'm going to talk about body image.

But you probably think that means I'm going to say things like...

you're beautiful just the way you are.

what you look like doesn't matter.

it's what's on the inside that counts.

if you love yourself, it shouldn't matter what other people think.

But...

this isn't a book about that.

You might believe all those things about other people, but you might not believe them about...

yourself.

You might hate the
way you sweat.

You might hate the way
you look in the mirror.

You might hate the
way your clothes fit.

You might hate the
size of your feet.

You might hate the
shape of your arms.

You might hate
your body.

I've been there too.

And I still am sometimes.

You see, I'm big.

Like, really big.

I'm taller than average,

but what makes me
really big is...

I'm fat.

OK.

You might have heard calling someone "fat" is mean. That it's wrong.

And that definitely can be true. Some people call other people "fat" because they want to hurt their feelings.

That is sooooooooooo not cool. Don't do that.

But when I call myself "fat",
I'm not being mean to myself.
I don't think being fat is a
bad thing anymore...

being fat is just part of
who I am.

I'm also white.

I have blonde-ish hair
and green eyes.

I wear glasses and I walk
around with my dog a lot.

I'm usually smiling, but
sometimes I'm not.

I wear jeans.

I wear dresses.

I wear sneakers.

I wear high heels.

I wear bright colors.

I wear lots of black.

But...

when people see me on the
street, the first thing
they notice about
me is how
fat I am.

I wish they noticed
my cute outfits or
my friendly smile,
but they don't.

And sometimes
when I notice them
noticing how fat I am,
I wish I could disappear.

Because even though I know...

I'm beautiful just the way I am...

what I look like doesn't matter...

it's what's on the inside that counts...

since I love myself, it shouldn't matter what other people think...

I still have days when I don't feel good about my body.

Days when I don't love my
body or myself.

You probably have days like that too.

Everyone does.

And I'm going to tell you why.

YOU DY?

What I'm about to tell you is kind of BIG.

IT'S

HU

There are a GAZILLION
companies and people
in the world who

claim they have products that will fix whatever is "wrong" with you.

They'll make your skin lighter.

They'll make your muscles bigger.

They'll make your hair straighter.

They'll make your teeth whiter.

They'll make you lose weight.

These companies would never make a single dollar if you didn't believe there was something about you that needed to be fixed.

So they spend LOTS OF MONEY
on advertisements to make you think
that if you buy their stuff,
you'll become
a little smaller,
a little more attractive,
a little stronger,
and all of your problems will go away.

Here's the real truth:

nothing about you needs
to be fixed.

Your skin is the color it's supposed to be.

Your muscles are the size they're supposed to be.

Your hair is as curly as it's supposed to be.

Your teeth don't need to be any whiter than they already are.

And you don't need to lose weight.

Don't believe me?

Right now, your body is doing hundreds of things that let you think, feel, breathe, and live.

Your bones are growing, white blood cells are fighting off germs and viruses, your heart is pumping pints of blood all the way from your pinkie toes to your pinkie fingers.

Your body is amazing!

Check it out.

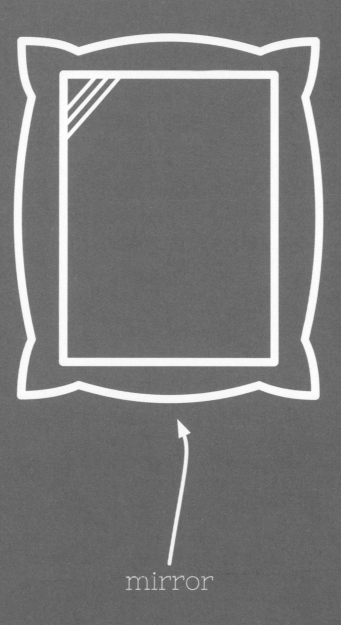

mirror

It is so good at stuff.

Scientists all over the world are trying to build robots and sensors and computers that do things as well as your body does them.

Your body is really freaking awesome.

And this very special body of yours can tell you what it needs.

Listen to it.

Let the voice that says, "I'm hungry," speak louder than the one that says, "I have to weigh less."

Let the voice that says, "That soccer game looks like fun," speak louder than the one that says, "But what if I get sweaty?"

Let the voice that says, "I really want to go swimming," speak louder than the one that says, "But what if people think I look funny?"

Think about all the great
things about you.

Maybe you're a really
fast runner.
Or you work hard.
Or can eat a lot of
chicken nuggets.
Or maybe you're the best video
game player in your whole class.
You're a really good friend.
You always have the best ideas.
You're trustworthy.
You can turn any bad day
into a good one.

(If you can't think of anything that is great about you, ask a grownup—they'll know!)

All these things matter a lot.
They make you, you!

They're far more important than how your eyebrows look, or whether you have a pimple.

So repeat after me...

I am
who I am
who I am who
I am who I am who I am
who I am...

Get it?!
You are you.
Love your body.
It's yours and it's the
only one you'll ever have.

Outro
for grownups

I'm so glad you stuck around to the end of this book. Body image is a tough subject and it probably brought up a lot of feelings. The most important thing for you to do right now is talk about those feelings with the kids in your life.

Talk about the feelings we have about our bodies until you laugh. Talk about them until you cry. Talk about the feelings we have about our bodies until you can share things you may have been holding back.

And then keep talking about body image.

Meanwhile, surround yourself and the kids in your life with diverse forms of beauty. Find models on social media who look like you and models who don't—and encourage your kid to appreciate and respect the difference. Watch TV and movies together starring people with all sorts of bodies. Share books that feature a diverse group of characters—those that remind you of yourself and those who don't.

And if you can't find any of these things,
I hope you make them.

About The Author

Rebecca Alexander (she/her) wrote this book for parents—parents who have lots of photos of their kids, but no photos of themselves. Rebecca knows that today's grownups struggle with body image almost as much as kids do.

But Rebecca's a believer. A believer in a future where people spend less time thinking and worrying about how they look. She likes to think about the world we could all build without these never-ending distractions. She imagines a world with public dance parties, people sun-bathing unapologetically in today's largely unused front yards, and communities where what makes people happy and satisfied is what matters most.

When Rebecca's not writing, she's building community with plus-size people through her company, AllGo, and on her little farm between Portland and the Oregon coast.

 @rebeccathefree　 @rebeccathefree　 rebeccathefree.com

Made to empower.

a kids book about **racism**
by Jelani Memory

a kids book about ANXIETY
by Ross Szabo

a kids book about DISABILITY
by Kristine Napper

a kids book about IMAGINATION
by LEVAR BURTON

a kids book about belonging
by Kevin Carroll

a kids book about failure
by Dr. Laymon Hicks

a kids book about GRATITUDE
by Ben Kenyon

a kids book about LIFE ONLINE
by Dave S. Anderson & Blake Fleischacker

a kids book about body image
by Rebecca Alexander

a kids book about IMMIGRATION
by MJ Calderon

a kids book about EMPATHY
by Daron K. Roberts

a kids book about GENDER
by Dale Mueller